NEW CRAFTS
PICTURE FRAMING

20 inspirational projects shown step by step

RIAN KANDUTH

PHOTOGRAPHY BY NICKI DOWEY

LORENZ BOOKS

This edition is published by Lorenz Books,
an imprint of Anness Publishing Ltd,
108 Great Russell Street,
London WC1B 3NA;
info@anness.com

www.lorenzbooks.com;
www.annesspublishing.com

If you like the images in this book and would like to investigate
using them for publishing, promotions or advertising, please visit
our website www.practicalpictures.com for more information.

© Anness Publishing Ltd 2014

A CIP catalogue record for this book
is available from the British Library.

Publisher: Joanna Lorenz
Project Editors: Doreen Palamartschuk-Gillon and Felicity Forster
Photographer: Nicki Dowey
Illustrators: Madeleine David, Vana Haggerty and Rob Highton
Designers: Lilian Lindblom and Lucy Doncaster
Production Controller: Mai-Ling Collyer

PUBLISHER'S NOTE
Although the advice and information in this book are believed to be
accurate and true at the time of going to press, neither the authors
nor the publisher can accept any legal responsibility or liability
for any errors or omissions that may have been made nor for any
inaccuracies nor for any loss, harm or injury that comes about from
following instructions or advice in this book.

Bracketed terms are intended for American readers.

CONTENTS

INTRODUCTION

Picture frames can be as eye-catching and interesting as the work they adorn. An imaginative well-made surround can enhance any image, be it a picture, photograph, textile or less conventional artwork, and throughout history, styles of frames have often reflected trends in art of the era. Making and decorating picture frames is a rewarding and challenging craft, and can be mastered quickly and successfully with a few basic carpentry techniques that guarantee professional-looking results. With the vast array of pre-cut wooden mouldings and mountboards available, the choice of which style of frame you can make is endless. There are also many pre-decorated mouldings on the market today, but often it is more enjoyable experimenting, devising and decorating your own individual frame.

Left: Frames with metallic finishes can be made by different methods, for example gilding, using metal paints or decorating with metal objects.

ORIGINS OF THE FRAME

Throughout history, picture frames have been an integral part of every household's inventory. Yet the frame is a curious object that is usually overlooked in the study of art. Picture framing is a skilful craft that has been in existence for hundreds of years. It is primarily concerned with the protection and preservation of artworks, but it also serves as a means of displaying pictures.

"A good picture deserves a good frame and a bad picture may sometimes preserve its place longer by having a handsome frame." (Charles Willson Peal *c*.1807)

Frames surrounding images have been an integral part of Western art since early Roman times and many Christian Byzantine mosaics had patterned borders.

In the Medieval period, during the 11th and 12th centuries, the frame was drawn as part of the picture. Monks added illuminated borders to their decorated manuscripts. Although such 'frames' were clearly separate from the text itself, the lettering used for the text often included aspects of the border design. Giotto's frescoes in Florence and Assisi had borders painted around them to separate scenes.

The first recorded wooden frames appeared during the 13th century, found in churches and cathedrals. They were designed by craftsmen who also created screens, pulpits and choirstalls. These frames often took the form of a 'triptych' – three panels of wood hinged together; the central panel held the main painting and the two side panels contained a design or painting complementary to it.

The paintings of this period were usually ecclesiastical and of icons or saints. The surrounding frame generally

Above: This 13th-century Italian painting of the Virgin Mary has a plain wooden frame.

Above: Jesus Christ on the cross and in six scenes of the Passion. Created c.1475 by Maître François, the ornate pillars and columns were painted on to make the frame.

Above: The Last Judgement *by Hieronymus Bosch (1450–1516) has a wooden triptych frame.*

included elements of architecture. One popular style during the 13th century was the 'tabernacle' frame, which incorporated pilasters and half columns.

During the 15th century, the Renaissance in Italy brought great changes in art and framing: as well as ecclesiastical paintings, wealthy patrons began to commission artists to execute portraits. Artists themselves were now beginning to recognize the frame as an important element in the pictures they were creating. As artists became more respected, they had less time to make their own frames, so this role frequently passed to furniture and cabinet makers. In this way, the separate craft of picture framing slowly emerged.

The changes that began in Italy spread to other parts of Europe. However, each country developed its own particular features. Germany concentrated on carving dense, crisp decoration, often ornamented with ivory inlays, shells, copper and semi-precious stones. Spain adopted a stronger, simpler, heavier ornamentation, and used a very dark tone for its gold leaf. Frames were now starting to take on a style inspired by ancient Greek architecture. As time progressed Italian frames became more elaborately carved and gilded.

During the 16th century, the focus of the arts was now switching from Italy to France, where Francis I (1515–47) invited Italian craftsmen and artists to Court. In England, the reign of Henry VIII (1509–47) also brought many foreign craftsmen as demand grew for paintings and frames, both for the great palace collections of the King and in private homes. After the Dissolution of the Monasteries, craftsmen went into secular service and found a market for their skills in private homes.

Above: Two carved, pierced and gilded Rococo frames from the 18th century decorated with shell themes, and in the centre, a faux tortoiseshell frame with ebony.

There was an ongoing battle between Henry VIII and Francis, as each attempted to out-do the other in terms of artistic style and opulence.

The frame became increasingly ornate during the late 17th and 18th centuries, firstly with the highly decorative Baroque style and then in the Rococo style. This reflected the trends in painting and, even more importantly, the decorative arts during the period.

Craftsmen required a great degree of skill to produce these elaborate frames. The popularity of such extravagant styles decreased progressively, and there was a gradual return to simpler, more austere frames. Toward the end of the 18th century, geometric forms again became fashionable. In 1758, the English Adam brothers visited Italy frequently, returning with detailed studies of ancient Roman and Greek architecture. In spite of the spreading influence of the French, their classical style became a major influence in picture frame making.

Above: Four 14th-century Spanish frames. Left to right: a frame painted flat with a deeply cut scrolled corner ornament and a raised inner profile; two gilded drawing frames, one with a marbled fascia to the outer edge and the other with a leaf-embellished ogee to the inner; a darkly gilded frame.

Above: A late 17th-century design for a mirror frame, with mythological figures and allegory by Andrea Brustolon (1662–1732).

Above: The Archduke Leopold William, Governor of Flanders, in his art gallery – a painting that depicts contemporary styles of frames. Painted by David Teniers II, a Flemish artist (1610–90).

Dutch frames had their own individual development, especially during the 17th century, although their original inspiration had also been the Italian Renaissance. Dutch artists and framemakers often painted the frames black with very little use of gilding or colouring. Dutch merchant shippers had begun to import ebony and other exotic woods, which inspired framemakers to experiment and use veneers of wood, tortoiseshell and turtleshell.

At the end of the 17th century, the influx of the Huguenots in England brought the talent and the influence of their carvers, gilders and cabinetmakers from France. At the same time, rulers William and Mary favoured Dutch designs. Oval frames appeared and were

Above: An oval frame surrounds this portrait of Madememoiselle Desmares, an actress with the Comédie Française, c.1720–30.

popularly used for portraits. In 1733, the duty on imported timber was abolished, and mahogany became fashionable. One can still find mahogany frames of this period, but they are becoming very rare.

Once again, Italy set the style at the end of the 18th century – a more severe style of decoration was in vogue, known as Neo-Classicism, in reaction to the extravagant taste of the previous movements. In France, Louis XVI frames were of a plainer geometric form, frequently rectangular or oval, some surmounted by crowns or wreaths. During the reign of Napoleon Bonaparte, at the beginning of the 19th century, a love of uniformity arose. The 'Empire' frame consisted of plaster motifs derived from palm leaves, lotus and papyrus, an Egyptian influence, as well as classic forms.

'Composition' frames were introduced at the start of the 19th century, and began to replace the traditional carved wood as a material. Whiting, resin and size (animal glue) were heated, amalgamated and pressed into moulds of boxwood and left to set, and then the ornament was applied to a basic wooden profile. Frames could be produced much quicker and became less

Above: A composition frame decorated with celestial bosses, and an English 19th-century frame carved, pierced and overpainted in the style of Grinling Gibbons, and decorated with scrolling acanthus leaves, flowers and grapes.

Above: Two French Louis XVI carved and gilded oval frames with shot and lamb's tongue ornament to the edges and ribbon-tied crests. The centre frame is a French Louis XVI carved and gilded frame; the ogee knull has a decorative leaf and crest.

expensive than individually carved frames. In England, during the Victorian period, Rococo imitations were prevalent until the 1880s, when there was a revival of Neo-Classicism and of the Adam brothers' designs. The oval was revived and at the end of the century Art Nouveau appeared with Oriental influences.

In efforts to break from the past, the 21st century has seen many experiments in framing. Presently, most frames are quite plain. However, re-creations of the elaborately carved and gilded frames of the past are occasionally seen. Highly skilled wood carvers and gilders still exist, although there are fewer than in previous times. The history of picture framing, like so much else in history, is cyclical: styles come and go, and return again.

Above: An early 20th-century French frame with Art Nouveau motifs showing a family portrait.

GALLERY

The frame is often considered to be secondary to the work that it encloses. However, a frame, be it understated or elaborate, can have a huge impact – both favourable and unfortunate – on the artwork itself. The following pages show the decorative scope employed by contemporary framemakers, from minimalist or natural finishes to highly ornate carved and gilded examples.

*Above: LARGE MANUFACTURED SWEPT FRAME
This frame incorporates silver beading on the rebate and outside edges to complement the dark silver grey face. The moulding is wide and deep, and the aperture for the mirror is small.
Rian Kanduth*

*Left: LARGE HOCKEY OR HALF-ROUND FRAME
Made of obeche wood, this frame is decorated with decoupage. The paper was stained with dilute burnt sienna gouache paint, before being protected with shellac. Frame by Rian Kanduth; collection of Maggie and Dennis Jakeman*

*Above: SMALL CUT BACK ASH FRAME
This frame has a dark grey wood stain finish, protected with clear wax. Since the ash frame is designed for three-dimensional objects, small wooden fillets were inserted to prevent the glass touching the artwork. Artwork and frame by Rian Kanduth*

Left: CROSS-OVER FRAME
The colour of the oak frame was heightened using a dark oak stain. It houses a double-thickness single window mount. This type of mount gives an unusual amount of depth on the bevel, but it is difficult to cut accurately. Frame by Rian Kanduth; picture by Andy Kingsbury

Below: SMALL HOCKEY FRAMES
These pine frames have been water-gilded using an assortment of yellow and white gold leaf. Some of the frames have been distressed with pumice powder. The white gold leaf was left to tarnish for eight months. Rian Kanduth

Right: LARGE ASH CUSHION FRAME *(left)* and SMALL FLAT-FACED ASH FRAME
These two natural wood frames were carefully sanded to produce a smooth finish. The flat-faced frame was left untreated, while the cushion frame was finished with several coats of clear wax. Rian Kanduth

Below: MOSAIC MIRROR
The shape of this frame has Arabic influences, with a domed-shaped top. The background of the frame is painted with aquamarine emulsion. Clear safety glass was arranged on the surface and grouted. The colour shows through the glass to create an even mosaic finish.
Dee Morgan

Right: WAVY MOULDING
The pine frame has been stained dark mahogany and contains a black single window mount. The picture itself is extremely small and would be lost in a large mount or a small moulding. With this combination, the frame draws the eye inwards towards the photograph.
Rian Kanduth

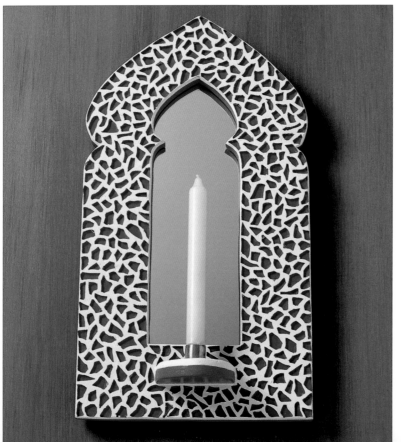

Above: SMALL HOCKEY FRAME
This frame was made from ramin, a very straight and close-grained wood, and stained with dilute grey wood stain. A stepped mount breaks up the large area of whiteness surrounding the artwork.
Rian Kanduth

Opposite: STEPPED MOULDING (top) and LARGE FLAT FACE FRAME
Both obeche frames have been water-gilded on black bole. The stepped moulding was gilded with gold leaf, and the white gold leaf frame was left to tarnish. Leonard Villa Framemakers and Gilders, and Rian Kanduth

Left: CASSETTA FRAME
This frame has been water-gilded using white gold leaf on blue bole, with the central section hand-painted in black gouache paint. The deckle-edged picture was positioned on white card, leaving a narrow edge all around so that the bevel of the stepped window mount holds the card rather than the picture. Frame by Rian Kanduth; picture by Neil Park; collection of Andrew Jakeman

Above: CARVED FRENCH WALNUT FRAME
This frame was hand-carved, and incorporates rann d'el foliage *design on either side of the face and scrollwork, and a stylized flower design on the horizontals. Frame carved by Robert Randall*

Left: HAND-BUILT STEPPED FRAME
This frame has been water-gilded using white gold leaf on brown bole. The narrow fillets are also water-gilded. The window mount is stepped as well as embossed. Frame by Leonard Villa Framemakers and Gilders; picture by Andy Kingsbury

Above: MEDIUM FLAT-FACED FRAME
This ash frame has been left in its natural state so as not to overpower the detailed deckle-edged artwork. White-painted wooden fillets were used to raise the glass above the artwork. Frame by Rian Kanduth; picture by Damien Sell

Left: CARVED OAK FRAME
This hand-carved frame incorporates Grinling Gibbons-style foliage, grapes and husks, with acanthus leaves in the corners. The wood has been left untreated. Frame carved by Ashley Sands

Above: LARGE HALF-ROUND FRAME
This ash frame has been stained dark oak and incorporates white fillets. The picture has been laid on silk mountboard. Rian Kanduth

MATERIALS

The materials listed below are fairly inexpensive, and the majority can be purchased at art stores, hardware stores and builders' merchants. However, gold leaf is expensive. It is advisable to practise with a cheaper type of leaf, such as Dutch metal leaf, which comes in various colours. When proficient in handling the leaf, graduate to real gold leaf.

Abrasive paper Available in different grades from fine to coarse. Wet and dry abrasive paper is the most economical type as it is reusable.

Acrylic gesso Used to provide a very smooth base to a frame. It can be sanded to porcelain smoothness.

Acrylic varnish Available in different sheens from high gloss to matt (flat). Acrylic varnish has a much faster drying time than spirit- (alcohol-) based varnishes and is more pleasant to work with. Craquelure is a two-part varnish, available at most art stores, which produces a crackled effect.

Backing tape Applied to the back of the frame and hardboard to cover the pins and to prevent dust entering. The self-adhesive type is recommended.

Barrier board Available in various colours and pH values (pH7 is neutral, pH below 7 is acidic, pH above 7 is alkaline). For the protection of artwork it is advisable to use a neutral pH.

Birch-faced plywood sheet A construction material consisting of thin sheets of wood glued together. The woodgrains of adjacent sheets are arranged at right angles to each other, which makes the plywood exceptionally strong for its light weight. It has an unusual and pleasing pattern.

Cloth Useful for applying oil or oil paints, and for cleaning glass.

Cork sanding block This tool is useful when sanding flat surfaces, as it will help to avoid making dips in the surface.

Danish oil Applied to unprimed wood, this will slightly darken the wood and will result in a natural sheen.

Epoxy resin glue A very strong adhesive used in framing with metal, stone or glass.

Etching spray Used for creating patterns on glass; available at most good art stores.

Fillet A thin length of wood used to separate glass from artwork or when framing a canvas.

Fine black felt-tipped pen Used for marking glass when measuring and cutting.

Gaffer tape Exceptionally strong industrial tape, available from most hardware stores.

Gelatine capsules When melted in hot water, these capsules produce an adhering solution for use in verre eglomisé.

Glass Picture glass is usually 2mm (⅛in) thick and up to 1m (3ft) long. Larger pieces of glass are more dense, about 4–6mm (¼in) thick. Museum glass is extremely expensive, but for precious artwork it is recommended. Non-reflective glass has a cloudy etched look and can be quite distracting.

Gold and silver leaf Numerous sorts of leaf are available. Gold is very expensive; Dutch metal or silver leaf are cheaper alternatives. Leaf is available either loose or on transfer sheets.

Gouache paint A water-based paint, more opaque and economical than watercolour paints. Gouache paint is obtainable at all good art stores.

Hardboard Several types and thicknesses of hardboard are available. The most commonly used is 3mm (⅛in) thick.

Lacquer There are various types of lacquer available, both water-based and spirit-based. Acrylic varnish is used in wood staining.

Lime wax This consists of clear wax with whiting that collects in the grain of the wood and results in a pale limed effect.

Metal foils Thin sheets of copper, brass and aluminium, available in art stores.

Metal polish A very fine abrasive cream. It may be used for any shellac-based project to give the frame's surface a glossy appearance.

Methylated spirits (methyl alcohol) This solvent is used as a thinner for wood stain and to clean paintbrushes.

Mounting (mat) board There is a wide range of mounting card available, falling mainly into two categories, regular and conservation. Conservation mounting card is acid-free.

Nylon thread Available from most haberdashery (notions) and fishing stores.

Oil size for gilding Available at any good art store, and used in oil gilding as a mordant. It is available with different drying times: the longer the drying time, the shinier the gold leaf.

Paints Gouache paint is very opaque and economical and gives a professional finish. Acrylic paints are more translucent than gouache paint, and less expensive. Oil paints can also be used as a finish.

Pigments These are the purest form of paint and are extremely strong.

Pumice powder A powder abrasive used in this book for distressing verre eglomisé. Different grades are available.

Rotring pen Used for fine penwork.

Self-adhesive lead Available in different widths and sold in most hardware stores.

Shellac Also known as special pale polish and used on wood.

Silk screen cleaner Available at specialist art stores.

Spatula A small spatula is extremely useful for filling in mitres on the frame and for mixing epoxy resin glue.

Spray lacquer Available in black and clear at car stores. It is vital that lacquer is used carefully in a well-ventilated area. Always wear a safety mask.

Stencil card Thin card (stock) treated to make it strong and reusable.

Tape There are various self-adhesive tapes available for taping up the back of a frame. Double-sided tape may be used with small frames to secure fillets.

Teak oil A darkish oil for use on unprimed wood. It results in a natural warm sheen.

Tracing paper Used to copy designs and transfer them on to a frame.

Wax Clear wax is used to coat and enrich different types of wood.

White chinagraph pencil An erasable pencil used to mark metal, plastics, dark fabrics or glass temporarily.

White spirit (alcohol) This solvent is used for oil size, and for cleaning brushes when using oil-based products.

Wire (steel) wool Used for sanding and scoring surfaces, and for applying liming wax.

Wood glue PVA (white) wood glue is used for securing all wood.

Wood oil Danish and teak oil are applied to unprimed wood. Linseed oil may also be used, but it is not as dark as Danish or teak oil. All oils absorb into the wood, and some take longer than others to dry; follow the manufacturer's instructions.

Wood filler Used to fill in gaps on mitred corners and after punching nails into wood. Various types of filler are available in DIY stores.

Wood stain Available in an abundance of colours and types, from crystals to solutions. Wood stain can be bought from art stores and hardware stores.

Key
1 Pigments
2 Metal finish
3 Cotton and wire (steel) wool
4 Craquelure varnish
5 Methylated spirits (methyl alcohol)
6 Interior filler
7 Etching spray
8 Metal foils
9 Hardboard/barrier board
10 Mounting (mat) board
11 Oil paints
12 Gouache paint/ watercolour
13 White spirit (alcohol)
14 Self-adhesive lead
15 Glue and lacquer
16 Masking tape and backing tape
17 Epoxy resin glue
18 Cork sanding block
19 Gold leaf
20 Abrasive paper
21 Wood stains
22 Clear wax
23 Sewing needles
24 Velvet
25 Lime wax
26 Rotring pen/ chinagraph pencil/ spatulas
27 Cloth

EQUIPMENT

Some of the equipment listed below is basic frame-making equipment, which you will use again and again. Other items, for example the gilding tools, are only required for particular projects. Specialist tools, such as a framer's pin gun, are available from framing suppliers.

Blade Required for mount cutting to release the cut corners of the window mount to avoid tearing.

Bradawl or awl Used for making initial holes in hardboard or wood.

Burnishing tool Used to polish raised areas of a metal finish.

Clamps These come in all shapes and sizes and have various uses. A mitre clamp is a metal fixture, usually bolted to a work bench, in which moulding lengths are inserted and cut at a 45-degree angle.

Craft (utility) knife This has multiple uses in picture framing. There are several types so choose one that feels comfortable.

Cutting mat Essential for cutting on, as it protects the underlying surface.

Drill and drill bits Both electric and hand drills are suitable.

D-rings There is a vast range of hinges available. D-rings are available single or double (for larger frames). Attach them to the hardboard with butterflies (rivet-like fixings), or screw directly into the back of the frame.

Framer's pin gun This tool is for fitting up picture frames. It inserts flat pins into the moulding, which hold the hardboard securely in place.

Gilder's cushion Gold leaf is laid on top of this before being cut.

Gilder's knife A special knife used for cutting gold leaf.

Gilder's tip Used for picking up gold leaf and applying it to the surface.

Glass cutter Diamond-headed and tungsten types for heavy-duty glass cutting can be quite expensive. There are cheaper alternatives for domestic use.

Hacksaw Used in a mitre clamp to cut wooden or manufactured mouldings. There are various types of saw blade, including blades for cutting metal mouldings.

Hand-held underpinner tool This has many uses. When joining the frame it acts as a hand-held underpinner, pushing 'V' pins into the joined mitre cuts and holding the frame together. It is also capable of securing the hardboard to the frame.

Heatgun An electrical appliance used for burning in patterns in wooden mouldings.

Mitre box A box for cutting moulding lengths at a 45-degree angle.

Mitre clamp A metal fixture, usually bolted to a bench, into which mouldings are inserted and cut at a 45-degree angle.

Mount cutter A tool for cutting a bevelled window out of mounting board. Buy hand-held ones at good art stores.

Paintbrushes Use flat-face oil and sable brushes, about 1cm (½in) and 2.5cm (1in) wide for detailing and pointing. Use stencil brushes for stencilling.

Panel pins (brads) Thin pins used for joining frames and tacking hardboard to a frame in the final assembly stage; an alternative to the hand-held underpinner.

Safety gloves Use rubber gloves for painting, and protective gloves for metal foils and when cutting glass.

Safety mask Wear when using any sprays to avoid inhalation.

Straight edge rule Akin to a ruler, this tool is more industrial.

Tack hammer A lightweight hammer used for joining frames.

Tape measure Used for measuring artwork, mounts and moulding.

Tenon saw A 30cm- (12in-) wide, flat saw used with a mitre box to cut wooden or manufactured mouldings.

T-square A measuring tool used to give a true square or rectangle. Used when measuring mounts and cutting glass.

'V' pins Used with the hand-held underpinner tool to underpin the frame.

Wire cutters Used to cut metal foil and hanging wire.

Key
1 Mitre clamp
2 Hacksaw
3 Safety gloves
4 Tenon saw
5 Mitre box
6 Drill and bits
7 Heatgun
8 Safety mask
9 G-clamp
10 T-square
11 Framer's pin gun
12 Straight edge rule
13 Clamp
14 Gilder's cushion and knife
15 Paintbrushes
16 Gilder's tip
17 Stencil brush
18 Ruler/hand-held under-pinner tool/craft (utility) knife/glass cutter/ 'V'-pins
19 Tape measure/ eraser/blade/ cutting mat
20 Tack hammer
21 Mount cutter
22 Rubber gloves
23 Wire cutters
24 Plastic burnishing tool/bradawl or awl/ burnishing tool

BASIC TECHNIQUES

The techniques used throughout this book are not difficult to learn, and can be easily mastered after a little practice. It is very important to take precise measurements, and it is often worthwhile double-checking your measurements before you cut anything. Once you have made your frame, choose a suitable place to hang it, and the best fixings to use for each kind.

MEASURING A PICTURE FOR A MOUNT

The primary purpose of a mount is to separate the artwork from the glass. Since paper fibres tend to expand and contract with temperature and humidity changes, which results in buckling or waving of the artwork, the mount allows room for movement inside the frame. The wide range of mounting (mat) boards available fall mainly into two categories, regular and conservation. Regular boards become acidic over the years and can damage your artwork. Conservation boards are acid-free and will not damage artwork. Where a mount is not used, it is recommended that fillets are used to prevent the glass from touching the artwork.

The mount must always be larger than the artwork. It is customary to allow a larger margin at the bottom of the mount than at the top or the sides to correct an optical illusion that occurs when the picture is hung on the wall. If all the margins were the same width, the bottom one would appear smaller than the others.

1 Measure the picture horizontally, and add on 7.5cm (3in) to both sides. This will give you the landscape measurement.

2 Measure the picture vertically, adding on 7.5cm (3in) at the top and 8.5cm (3½in) at the bottom. This will give you the portrait measurement (see diagram for guide).

3 Following the measurements, cut the mounting board to size. Mark inner measurements on to the mounting board using the tape measure. Join up the measurements with a ruler and pencil to mark the pencilled window.

4 Line up the straight edge against the edge of the mount, push the mount cutter blade into the board and move the mount cutter steadily along the marked line to cut out the window. Go over the pencil mark crossovers slightly, to avoid cross-cuts on the face of the mount.

Landscape 14in (35cm)

7.5cm (3in)

7.5cm (3in)

7.5cm (3in)

7.5cm (3in)

8.5cm (3½in)

Landscape 14in (35cm)

Pencil mark measurements and crossovers

5 Once you have cut out the window, carefully place a blade into each corner and trim the cut edge to release the centre freely. This will avoid any tearing of the corners. Erase the pencil marks.

6 Place the window mount face up on the picture below it, and line them up. Attach the picture to the mount using acid-free hinging tape on the top edges of the artwork.

TRACING PATTERNS

flat front section

bevel (cross-section)

LAY-ON MOUNT

mounting (mat) board

artwork

artwork

mounting board (uncut)

BOOK MOUNT

back of mount

adhesive tape

adhesive hinges

mounting board (uncut)

FLOAT MOUNT

back of artwork

adhesive tape

gap all around artwork

artwork

front mount

adhesive tape

mounting board (uncut)

back section

CUTTING AND JOINING A FRAME

There are several ways of cutting a section of moulding, using either a mitre clamp or a wooden mitre box. When joining the frame, a few basic tools are required: a vice, a frame clamp, a hand-held underpinner tool and a framer's pin gun.

1 Measure the artwork for the mount to give you the inside rebate (rabbet) measurement for the frame. Start by cutting the moulding length at a 45-degree angle, as shown. The edge of the moulding with the rebate should be the furthest from you.

2 Measure along the inside rebate of the moulding and mark the first cut on the face of the moulding.

3 Insert the moulding into the mitre clamp or box and cut with a saw at a 45-degree angle.

4 Place the moulding in the mitre clamp or box. To make the next section of the frame, cut away the triangle 'offcut' as in step 1 with the same 45-degree angle. Do this before you measure the second cut.

5 Measure and mark the second cut on the moulding. Repeat the above steps until all four lengths are cut. To check that they are the correct length, hold them together and place your fingertips on the edges of the cuts. They should feel flush.

6 Using PVA (white) wood glue, stick two sections of the moulding together to make a right angle. Repeat with the other sections, then join them all together to make the frame.

7 Place the frame clamp round the frame to hold the glued pieces together. Wipe away excess PVA glue with a damp cloth. Be sure to clean off excess glue otherwise colourwash or wood stain will not take to the wood.

8 Once the frame is secured in the frame clamp, turn the frame face down, then place underpins into the corners of the back of the frame using a hand-held underpinner tool. Or, place the right-angled corners of the frame in a vice, and hammer panel pins (brads) into the corner edges of the moulding using a tack hammer. Once all four corners have been pinned, leave overnight to dry.

9 Turn the frame right side up and fill in the mitred corners with wood filler. Wipe away excess wood filler with a damp cloth.

10 Once the wood filler has set (the time taken will vary depending on the type of filler you use, but usually it will be an hour or so), use a cork sanding block and coarse-grade abrasive paper to sand all over the frame and the rebate. Repeat with finer-grade abrasive paper.

GLASS CUTTING

There are various types and thicknesses of picture glass available. Picture glass is usually thinner than window glass, and without flaws. Glass is required on any artwork needing protection from atmospheric pollution and ultraviolet rays, which in time will cause a picture to fade. The most commonly used glass is 2mm (⅛in) clear glass. For more precious artwork, museum glass is used; although extremely expensive, it is undoubtedly the best protection for artwork and it is almost invisible. Non-reflective glass has a cloudy etched appearance. For reasons of safety, 2mm (⅛in) glass is used only up to a certain size, about 1m (3ft). For areas larger than this, over-sized heavy duty 4–6mm (¼in) glass should be used or, alternatively, Perspex (Plexiglas) may be substituted.

2 Reduce this measurement by 3mm (⅛in), then mark the measurement on the glass using a fine black felt-tipped pen.

4 Holding the glass carefully over a board so that the score line is along the edge of the board, gently tap the glass below the score mark, using the round end of the cutter.

1 Measure the artwork for the mount to give you the inside rebate (rabbet) measurement for the frame. Start by cutting the moulding length at a 45-degree angle, as shown. The edge of the moulding with the rebate should be the furthest from you.

3 Place a T-square on the glass and line up the glass cutter so that it is on top of the marks. Holding both the glass cutter and T-square, firmly but gently score the glass in one long smooth stroke using the glass cutter. Do not cut over the same cut, as this will make the glass shatter and splinter.

5 Place a pencil directly beneath the cut. Using both hands placed on either side of the pencil and score mark, gently but firmly press the glass down. The glass will break cleanly along the score line.

6 Repeat steps 1–5 for the vertical measurement on the glass.

7 When the glass is cut, gently insert it in the rebate at the back of the frame.

ASSEMBLING A FRAME

'Fitting up' is the process of fixing the artwork into the frame itself. It is advisable to follow the simple steps below and assemble the sections in the correct order.

1 Measure the artwork then measure and cut the mount. Adhere the artwork by hinging it to the back of the mounting board as in this single window mount. Cut out the barrier board and hardboard and place these beneath the mounted board. Measure the inside rebate, vertical and horizontal. Mark and cut the glass to the correct size.

2 Place the glass on a soft white background (to see dust and dirt), and clean with a soft cloth and methylated spirits (methyl alcohol). Place the artwork, barrier board and hard board below the clean glass.

3 Carefully place the frame over the glass, artwork, barrier board and hardboard. Hold up the frame and layers vertically and check for dust.

4 Remove the hardboard from the back of the frame, keeping the other layers together. Make two level holes in the hardboard with a bradawl or awl, not too close either to the centre or to the edge of the hardboard. Place D-rings on top of the holes and insert a butterfly rivet through the hole of the D-ring and the hole in the hardboard.

5 Turn the hardboard over (reverse or non-wall side showing), place a nail punch (or a long nail) between the 'wings' of the butterfly and hammer on the nail punch. This will open the butterfly. Once opened, hammer the butterfly fully open and flat.

6 Turn the hardboard over, (front or wall side showing) and insert the picture cord through the D-rings, wrapping it around each D-ring twice.

7 Tie the picture cord securely using overhand knots, about four knots on each side. If the picture is over 60cm (2ft) in length or height, it is advisable to use a cow hitch knot in the first D-ring. This type of knot will double up the picture cord, enabling it to take more weight. Use five or six overhand knots in the second D-ring.

8 Turn the frame over and put the hardboard in place over the back of the frame. Hold down the frame at the corners with one hand and use the pin gun with the other hand. This safeguards the mitred corners from popping open. Secure the frame layers by using the framer's pin gun to insert flat pins into the frame, as shown. An alternative way of pinning in the hardboard is by using panel pins (brads) and a tack hammer; place the pins flat on the hardboard and hammer them part of the way into the moulding as for the gun pins.

9 Place backing tape on the back of the frame, not too close to the edge of the frame, about 3mm (⅛in) away, otherwise the tape may be visible once the picture is hanging on the wall. Cut the tape with a craft (utility) knife down the outer edge of the frame, then fold the tape down.

cow hitch knot

overhand knot

D-ring

10 Using the craft knife, cut neat mitres in the backing tape on all four corners. Cut the tape where it covers both the hardboard and the moulding.

11 Remove the excess tape from both sides of each mitred corner.

12 Turn the frame face up and clean the glass with methylated spirits (methyl alcohol) and a soft cloth. Polish up the frame using a separate cloth.

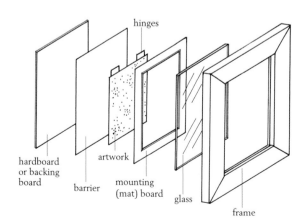

ORDER OF FITTING UP FOR WINDOW MOUNTS

hinges

hardboard or backing board

barrier

artwork

mounting (mat) board

glass

frame

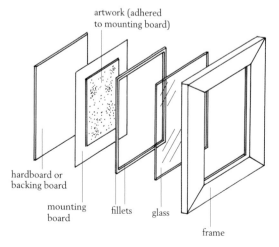

ORDER OF FITTING UP FOR LAY-ON OR DIMENSIONAL OBJECTS

artwork (adhered to mounting board)

hardboard or backing board

mounting board

fillets

glass

frame

MOULDINGS

Moulding is the shaped wood that will ultimately be composed into the frame itself. Mouldings are referred to by their profile, ie the cross-section or end-view. Mouldings are usually sold in 1.8m or 2.4m (6ft or 8ft) lengths, from a builders' merchant, timber yard, specialist art store or framer.

There are two basic types of moulding: picture frame moulding and builders' moulding. The principal contrast between the two is that picture frame moulding includes a fitted rebate (rabbet), a step that allows the artwork, mount, glass and hardboard to fit uniformly into place without collapsing through the frame. Builders' moulding is fundamentally intended for trimming internal structures such as door frames, windows and skirting boards, and consequently does not incorporate a fitted rebate. To convert builders' moulding it is necessary to create a recess by sticking a narrow strip of wood such as a fillet underneath the moulding.

Manufactured moulding is pre-decorated and finished. There is an impressive array of manufactured mouldings available, from reproduction, antiqued, metal and highly decorated to plain, simple styles.

Natural wood mouldings leave the embellishment in the hands of the framer. Ash and oak have a pleasing grain, and lime-waxing and wood staining these types of wood bring out the best of the natural grain. Obeche and ramin are woods that are suitable for more opaque or solid decoration. One factor to take into consideration is whether the wood is a softwood or a hardwood. For example, ash and oak are very hard and require some perseverance to cut, whereas obeche, pine and ramin are fairly easy to cut.

MANUFACTURED MOULDINGS

Key
1 Medium plain shaped moulding
2 Medium shaped moulding, with beading on the rebate (rabbet) edge
3 Large shaped moulding, with gold and silver finish
4 Large reverse moulding, with gold finish
5 Large foliage and waterleaf moulding, with gold finish
6 Large foliage moulding, with lacquer finish

PARTS OF A MOULDING

side edge

beading

inside edge
(sight size)

rebate
(rabbet)

TYPES OF MOULDINGS

medium hockey

small hockey

small flat face

medium flat face

large flat face (bevel)

slope

scoop

NATURAL WOOD MOULDINGS

NATURAL WOOD MOULDINGS

Key
1 Small flat face – pine
2 Medium hockey/cushion – ash
3 Medium flat face – oak
4 Small swept – obeche
5 Large swept – maple veneer
6 Large flat-face angled bevel – ramin
7 Large reverse moulding – ramin
8 & 9 Large plain cassetta – obeche

Key
1 Reverse moulding – oak
2 Cassetta – obeche
3 Cassetta – ramin
4 Swept obeche MDF (medium density fiberboard), compressed decoration
5 Large shaped ramin MDF, compressed decoration
6 Large wavy – pine
7 Large swept ramin MDF, compressed decoration

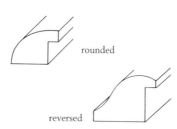

swept

angled

cut back angled

small cushion

rounded

reversed

two different
types of cassetta

FIXINGS

When hanging any artwork, it is vital to consider the weight and size of the frame. It is very easy to underestimate just how heavy a frame is, and therefore the type of fixings needed to hold it in place.

You can use wire or cord for hanging more or less any weight of frame. Single or double D-rings are sufficiently strong fixings for light to medium-weight frames, but you should use strap hangers for heavy or large frames.

Single and double D-rings can be inserted either into the hardboard using rivets or butterflies, or screwed directly into the back section of the frame. The wire or cord is threaded through the first fixing, using a cow hitch knot to secure, and then through the second fixing and secured using five or six overhand knots. Strap hangers are screwed on to the back section of the frame and wire or cord can be attached in the same way. However, if the frame is particularly heavy, it is recommended to hang the picture from the loops of the strap hanger on to screws inserted directly into the wall (rather than using picture wire or cord).

Anti-theft devices (ATDs) and mirror plates work in much the same way as strap hangers. The straight section is screwed into the back of the frame, and the curved section is screwed to the wall.

Spring clips can be used instead of pins to secure artwork in a frame. Their advantage is that they can easily be removed if you want to replace the artwork. The flat edge of the clip is screwed into the back of the moulding and the curled edge lies on top of the hardboard, securing the artwork within.

Key
1 Picture wire
2 Mirror plates
3 Anti-theft devices
4 Screws
5 Strap hanger
6 Double D-rings
7 Single D-rings
8 Rivets or butterflies
9 Picture cord
10 Spring clips

PICTURE HANGING

There are a few considerations to bear in mind when you are deciding where to hang a picture. Avoid placing artworks where fluctuating temperatures and humidity changes may be experienced, for example near a heat source or on an outside wall. Condensation encourages mould and may also cause the paper to buckle. It is also inadvisable to hang a painting of any kind in strong light or direct sunlight because of heat, dust and exposure to ultra-violet light. Ultra-violet rays damage artworks irrevocably and colours will fade in time if exposed to high levels of light. Paper tends to absorb high-energy photons from light, which in turn causes a chemical reaction in the paper, ultimately breaking it down and causing it to become brittle.

Never underestimate the weight of a frame. If it is heavy, it is best to insert screws into the wall and hang it directly from strap hangers screwed into the frame. Do not use cord or wire to hang heavy frames as these may give way under the weight.

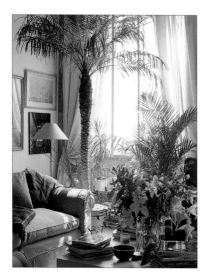

Above: A successful frame should enhance the work it frames without distracting from the image. In a living room, pictures may need to be hung at a slightly lower level than eye level, as you will most often be sitting down when looking at them.

Left: Pictures are an integral part of the decoration of your rooms. They should blend in with the interior, and you should take into account the light and colour scheme of the furniture and walls when you decide where to hang them. Pictures grouped together can look very effective.

Right: The image and frame of this picture enhance the atmosphere of the muted colour scheme of this room, with faded walls and washed floorboards.

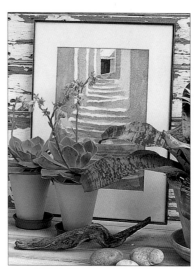

DECORATIVE WINDOW MOUNT

There is an abundance of decorative papers available, any of which may be cut into strips or abstract geometric shapes and used to transform a simple pre-cut mount into something special. Alternatively, you could cover the entire window mount in a single decorative paper, following the same technique for cutting and gluing that is used in the Velvet-covered Mount project.

1 On the face of the pre-cut window mount, mark out light lines with a pencil and ruler or straight edge, setting out where the decorative border is to be placed.

2 Place the decorative paper on a cutting mat to protect the surface and, using a craft knife and ruler, measure and cut the paper into appropriate-sized strips.

3 Apply spray mount or PVA glue on the reverse of the cut strips. Stick the strips to the markings on the face of the mount. Press down gently to secure.

4 Using a ruler and craft knife, carefully cut mitres on all four corners of the decorative strips. Remove excess paper once mitres have been cut.

Materials and Equipment You Will Need
Pre-cut mount • 2B (#2) soft pencil • Ruler or straight edge • Decorative paper • Cutting mat • Craft (utility) knife • Spray mount or PVA (white) glue

STEPPED WINDOW MOUNT

This design is similar to a normal single window mount but with the addition of a second mount, featuring a slightly larger window opening, stuck on top. This results in an interesting stepped look, and produces a stunning effect when made in different-coloured mounting board. You can experiment with all sorts of colour combinations to make even the most ordinary picture look good. The 'step' may be increased or decreased.

1 Measure the picture vertically and horizontally (see Basic Techniques). Following the measurements, cut two pieces of mounting board the same size. The size of the mount is a matter of personal preference.

2 Mark the measurements of the picture on one piece of board.

3 Then, on the other piece, mark the original measurements, but reducing the mount size by 1cm (½in). For example, if the original measurements are 7.5cm (3in) at the sides and top, and 8.5cm (3½in) at the bottom, the measurements on the other piece of board would be 6.5cm (2½in) for the sides and top, and 7.5cm (3in) at the bottom.

4 Erase the pencil marks and apply PVA glue on to the back of the reduced measurement mount. Place this on to the face of the original measurement mount. Press down to ensure good adhesion.

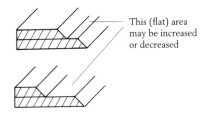

This (flat) area may be increased or decreased

Materials and Equipment You Will Need

Tape measure • Mount cutter • Cutting mat • 2 pieces of mounting board • 2B (#2) pencil • Straight edge • T-square • Blade • Eraser • PVA (white) glue and brush

VELVET-COVERED MOUNT

Fabric-covered mounts add an immense amount of richness and depth to an object or a picture, especially if you use a luxury fabric such as silk, brocade or velvet. In the past, Persian and Indian textiles were often framed by a fabric-covered mount. Be careful if you are using a thin fabric such as silk, as the glue may seep through the fabric, so only glue the overlaps on the reverse.

1 Place the pre-cut mount face down on to the velvet on a cutting mat. Leaving 2.5cm (1in) of fabric all around for overlaps, cut out the velvet with a craft knife.

2 Cut off the corners of the fabric to make folding over easier. Apply a thin, even coat of fabric glue to the face of the mount.

3 Place the fabric evenly on top of the mount, press down and rub gently with a cloth, or use a linoleum-cut roller to ensure good adhesion.

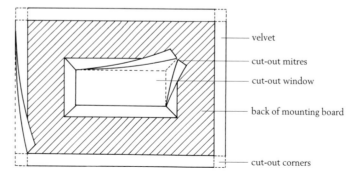

— velvet

— cut-out mitres

— cut-out window

— back of mounting board

— cut-out corners

Materials and Equipment You Will Need
Pre-cut mount · Velvet · Cutting mat · Craft (utility) knife · Ruler · Fabric glue and brush · Soft cloth or linoleum-cut roller

4 Turn over the covered mount so that the velvet fabric is face down. Cut a small square in the fabric in the window, leaving an extra amount of fabric for the overlaps.

5 Cut mitres in the overlap fabric in the window. Apply fabric glue on the mount where the overlaps will lie, then fold over the overlap fabric and press down firmly.

6 Fold down the overlaps on the side edges of the mount. At the corners, hold the velvet firmly and cut a mitre with a craft knife, then apply fabric glue and press the fabric down. Allow to dry.

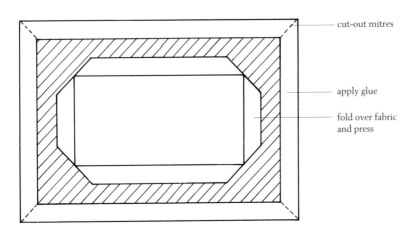

cut-out mitres

apply glue

fold over fabric and press

MULTIPLE WINDOW MOUNT

Sometimes more than one window mount is required, perhaps for a group of photographs or artworks, or to make a triptych. Cutting a multiple window mount is not an easy task to master at first; great care and concentration is needed when measuring and marking the artwork, and it is well worth double-checking your measurements before you make any cuts.

1 Place four pictures on a piece of mounting board. Mark the horizontal measurements of the top two and bottom two pictures in pencil, just touching the pictures on all sides.

2 Next mark the vertical measurements of the top and bottom pictures in pencil, again just touching the pictures on all sides.

3 Once measurements have been marked, join them up using a pencil and a ruler. Be sure to make crossovers, so when cutting the mount you will know where to stop.

Materials and Equipment You Will Need
Mounting (mat) board • 2B (#2) pencil • Tape measure • Ruler • T-square • Mount cutter • Cutting mat • Blade • Eraser • Acid-free hinging tape

4 Cut out the four windows, following the diagram below for the order of cutting. Move the mounting board as you work, so you are cutting vertically. Erase the pencil marks.

5 When all the windows have been cut, hinge the pictures as in a single mount (see Basic Techniques).

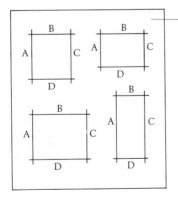

back of mount
with pencil marks

Cut in order of:
all A first
all B second
all C third
all D fourth

LIME-WAXED FRAME

Liming wax is a mixture of white pigment blended with clear wax, and is usually applied to wood with an attractive grain, such as oak or ash. The white pigment sits in the relief grain of the wood, while the raised grain remains beautifully translucent. This traditional technique is once again fashionable for kitchen doors and furniture, and it works equally well on a picture frame that will look right in many situations.

1 Sand the frame all over initially with coarse-grade, then with fine-grade abrasive paper for a smooth surface.

2 Using wire wool, pick up some liming wax from the tin and apply it to the frame in long even strokes, continuing all round the frame. Work the wax into the woodgrain as you go.

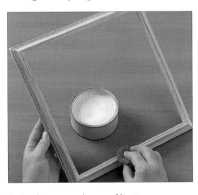

3 Apply a second coat of liming wax to achieve a deeper effect.

4 When you have covered the frame completely, gently polish the liming wax with a cloth. Do not use too much pressure as this will wipe off the previously applied wax.

Materials and Equipment You Will Need
Joined and sanded wooden frame • Coarse- and fine-grade abrasive paper • Wire (steel) wool • Liming wax • Cloth

PAINT-WASHED FRAME

Colourwashing involves using acrylic, emulsion (latex) or gouache paints. Depending on the density of the solution, the wash can be either translucent or opaque. The more translucent the wash, the more of the woodgrain will be apparent. Colourwashing is easily reversible by sanding off the colour, as it does not penetrate as deeply into the wood as wood stain.

1 Sand the frame. Place a walnut-sized amount of gouache paint into a bowl, add a small amount of water initially, and blend in thoroughly. The more water now added, the more translucent the wash will be; the less water added, the more opaque the wash will be. Test the strength of the wash on the back of the frame. Dip the paintbrush into the diluted water, then wipe the paintbrush on the side of the bowl, removing excess paint.

2 Apply the wash to one section of the face of the frame in one smooth even stroke, from mitre join to mitre join. Then paint the side section of the frame. Continue all around the frame. Leave to dry for at least 15 minutes. The more coats of wash, the more opaque the wood will appear. Two coats are recommended. Clean the brush thoroughly with water.

4 For a wax finish, cover your index finger with a cloth, dip it in wax and work it in on a small piece of hardboard (this will soften the wax and make it easier to use). With one long, smooth stroke, lightly apply the wax to the frame; do not rub it in as it may remove the wash. Continue all around the frame. Once finished, lightly rub in the wax from where you began. Two or three coats of wax may be applied for the required finish.

3 When the wash is completely dry, lightly sand the frame with fine-grade abrasive paper. This will slightly distress the wash and give a smooth finish.

Materials and Equipment You Will Need

Spectrum violet gouache paint • Glass bowl • 2.5cm (1in) flat sable paintbrush • Joined and sanded ash or oak frame • Fine-grade abrasive paper • Cloth • Clear wax • Hardboard offcut (scrap)

WOOD-STAINED FRAME

There is a wide variety of different wood stains on the market nowadays. The difference between a stain and a wash is that the stain will actually penetrate the wood significantly deeper than a wash, and will always let the grain of the wood show through. Brushes should be cleaned thoroughly when using a spirit-based stain, or water when using a water-based stain.

1 Sand the frame for a smooth finish. For an opaque result, use pure undiluted wood stain. For a more translucent finish, dilute the wood stain with methylated spirits or an appropriate solvent. Decant the mixture into a glass bowl. Wear rubber gloves when working with wood stain.

2 Dip the paintbrush into the solution, wiping the excess on the side of the bowl. Apply the stain to the face of the frame, from mitre to mitre, in one long, smooth, even stroke. Continue on to the side edge and then all around the frame. Leave to dry for 10–15 minutes.

4 When the wood stain is dry to the touch, apply a coat of acrylic varnish. Leave to dry before applying one or two more coats as required.

3 Two or three coats of wood stain may be required to achieve a deeper colour.

Materials and Equipment You Will Need
Abrasive paper • Frame • Spirit (alcohol-based) wood stain • Methylated spirits (methyl alcohol) • Glass bowl • Rubber gloves • 2.5cm (1in) flat sable paintbrush • Acrylic varnish

CRAQUELURE FRAME

Making a craquelure frame involves using a two-part varnish called craquelure. One is slow drying, while the other is fast drying. The varnish shrinks slightly as it dries, so as the slow-drying lower layer contracts, it causes cracking in the dry layer of varnish above. It is advisable to experiment with this technique, as timing and atmospheric conditions are important to achieve good results.

1 Using the flat sable paintbrush, apply four coats of white gouache paint to the frame, allowing each coat to dry for 5–10 minutes before applying the next. Once the gouache paint is dry, gently sand all around the frame using fine-grade abrasive paper. Spray the frame with clear spray lacquer to make the surface less absorbent.

2 Using the flat oil paintbrush, apply a coat of antiquing varnish sparingly over the frame and leave for 3 hours. The longer you leave the antiquing varnish to dry, the smaller the cracks will be.

3 When the varnish is slightly tacky, apply the craquelure glaze. Cracks will begin to appear in an hour or so, depending on the temperature of the room. It is best to leave the frame to dry overnight before continuing on to the next stage.

4 Once the cracks have appeared and the varnish is dry, place some olive green oil paint on a plate. Cover your index finger with a cloth and dip it into the oil paint. Apply the paint to the frame in strokes, working the colour into the cracks, until the frame is covered.

5 Continue around the frame, wiping the oil paint off with the cloth. This will remove the paint from the surface but leave the colour in the cracks.

Materials and Equipment You Will Need

2.5cm (1in) flat sable paintbrush • White gouache paint • Prepared and sanded frame • Fine-grade abrasive paper • Clear spray lacquer • 2.5cm (1in) flat oil paintbrush • Craquelure varnish • Olive green oil paint • Plate • Cloth

SCORCHED FRAME

This technique involves burning a design into the wood on the face or sides of the frame, or both, with a heatgun. A close-grained wood such as ramin is recommended; the more open-grained the wood, the greater the chance of the design spreading and blurring. It is best to use a simple, fairly large design. A metal foil template is used here, in the same way that you would use a cardboard template.

1 Draw your design on metal foil using a white chinagraph pencil. Cut out the design with a craft knife or wire cutters. Place your metal template on to the bare frame. Using the heatgun and wearing safety gloves, scorch the design into the wood, holding the heatgun 10–15cm (4–6in) away from the wood.

2 Using coarse-grade paper, sand off the over-burns. Repeat with fine-grade paper.

3 Mix raw sienna pigment with clear wax in the proportion of 1.5ml (¼ tsp) of pigment to 15ml (1 tbsp) of clear wax.

4 Apply the pigmented wax to the frame with a soft cloth. Work methodically all around the frame.

5 Using a dry, clean cloth, polish up the wax to a soft sheen.

Materials and Equipment You Will Need
Metal foil • White chinagraph pencil • Craft (utility) knife or wire cutters • Joined and sanded ash or oak frame • Heatgun • Safety gloves •
Coarse- and fine-grade abrasive paper • Raw sienna pigment • Clear wax • Soft cloths

RAISED MOTIF FRAME

Three-dimensional patterns applied on the face of a picture frame are simple to create with ordinary interior filler. The filler can be tinted any colour you choose by adding either pigment, gouache paint or watercolour paint and blending it in thoroughly. Alternatively, you can coat the entire frame with filler to achieve a plaster-like effect, and then place raised designs on top.

1 In a glass bowl, combine the cobalt blue gouache paint with water in the ratio of 1 part gouache paint to 3 parts water. Blend in well. Apply this wash on to the frame with the paintbrush in long, even strokes from mitre join to mitre join. Leave to dry for about 15 minutes.

2 Lightly distress the face and edges of the frame by rubbing with fine-grade abrasive paper all over.

3 Trace a design for the frame using the template at the back of the book, then transfer on to stencil card. Place this on a cutting mat and cut out the design with a craft knife.

4 Mix interior filler with water in the ratio of 2 parts filler to 1 part water, to achieve an ice cream consistency. Add paint or pigment to tint the filler. Place the stencil template on to the frame and hold it securely. Apply the filler with a stencil brush in a stippling motion.

5 Leave the interior filler to dry for about 30 minutes, then lightly sand with fine-grade abrasive paper.

Materials and Equipment You Will Need
Glass bowls • Cobalt blue gouache paint • Joined and sanded frame • 2.5cm (1in) flat sable paintbrush • Fine-grade abrasive paper • Tracing paper • Pencil • Stencil card • Cutting mat • Craft (utility) knife • Interior filler • Pigment • Stencil brush

FRAMED STONE

Birch-faced plywood sheet is used in this unusual frame because of its strength. The heavier the stone you wish to frame, the thicker the plywood needs to be. For a heavy stone, you will also need to replace the galvanized nails with strong screws. Use the frame to display a slab of stone carved with a hammer and chisel, as here, or alternatively painted or scratched with a design. When you are hanging a weighty piece of artwork such as this, it is advisable to use strap hangers and to hang it directly from screws in the wall, not on wire or cord.

1 Measure and saw the birch-faced plywood to fit the stone, allowing for a border about 4cm (1½in) all round. Using a drill with a masonry bit, drill four holes in the stone, one in each corner.

2 Sand the plywood first with coarse, then fine-grade abrasive paper, using a cork sanding block to smooth it down. Wearing rubber gloves, apply olive green oil paint with a soft cloth all over the plywood. Rub it well into the plywood. Buff with a clean, soft cloth.

3 Place the stone on to the plywood and level up. Place a cloth over the galvanized nails to avoid marking the stone when you hammer in through the drilled holes.

Materials and Equipment You Will Need
Tape measure • Tenon saw • 18mm (¾in) birch-faced plywood sheet • Drill • Masonry bit • Coarse and fine-grade abrasive paper •
Cork sanding block • Rubber gloves • Olive green oil paint • Soft cloths • 2.5cm (1in) galvanized nails • Tack hammer

METAL FOIL FRAME

This attractive frame incorporates two metal foils – one copper and one brass. You can also use other metal foils, such as aluminium or zinc. Working with metal foil gives plenty of opportunity for experimentation: shapes can be cut out and scored on the reverse side of the foil, for example, to give an embossed appearance on the front of the metal. The metal foil is quite easy to cut out using a knife.

1 Cut out a piece of copper foil (or pieces, as shown here) to fit over the frame, allowing for overlaps around the inner rebate (rabbet) and outer edge. Place the frame face down on the foil. Score the foil with a ballpoint pen around the inner rebate and outer edge. Remove the frame. Using a straight edge and a craft knife, cut out the corners on the outer edge in line with the score marks. Cut the inner rebate window and mitre the corners.

2 Fold the inner rebate foil around the moulding (see diagram). Tack it on to the frame with small brass pins, after making the initial holes with a bradawl or awl. Repeat on the outer edge. Place a brass pin in all four corners, where the foil will overlap.

3 Place the brass metal foil underneath the frame and fold it over, after making initial holes with the bradawl or awl, then pin. Hammer pins at the edges of the brass foil to create the design.

fold foil around inner rebate (rabbet)

Materials and Equipment You Will Need

Thin sheet of copper foil • Scissors or wire cutters • Prepared frame • Ballpoint pen • Straight edge • Craft (utility) knife • Cutting mat • Tack hammer • Brass escutcheon pins • Bradawl or awl • Brass metal foil • Wire (steel) wool • Protective gloves • Stencil card or aluminium metal foil • Black felt • White chinagraph pencil • Fabric glue and brush

4 Using wire wool and wearing protective gloves, score the copper foil in small circular motions.

5 Cut out a template using stencil card or aluminium foil. Place the template on the brass foil. Using wire wool, make small circular motions on the brass foil to score it.

6 Using a craft knife, cut out a piece of black felt to cover the back and edges of the frame, which are sharp. Mark an opening for the window with a white chinagraph pencil, then cut it out with a craft knife.

7 Coat the back of the frame with fabric glue, then place the piece of black felt on the glue.

8 Fold the edges of the felt into the back of the window, taking care not to overlap it on to the rebate.

DECOUPAGE FRAME

The art of paper decoration has existed since ancient times in many cultures, notably in China, Japan and Poland, and it reached a high point in 18th-century Europe. The word 'decoupage' comes from the French 'découper', meaning 'to cut up', and it is a technique using paper cut-outs to create scenes and designs on furniture, walls, screens and other articles. The paper cut-outs are painted, pasted on and then sealed with several coats of lacquer, which makes these paper decorations very hardwearing.

1 Using the 2.5cm (1in) flat sable paintbrush, apply acrylic gesso over the prepared frame. Allow to dry, then apply another four coats of gesso, allowing each coat to dry before applying the next. Once the acrylic gesso is completely dry, sand it down gently with fine-grade abrasive paper wrapped around a sanding block. Do not wet the abrasive paper.

2 Combine 1.5ml (¼ tsp) of yellow ochre pigment with 30ml (2 tbsp) of water and blend thoroughly until there are no flecks of pigment in the mixture. Using the flat sable paintbrush, apply two coats of the yellow ochre pigment mixture over the frame. Allow to dry.

3 Photocopy the designs you wish to use from a book or magazine. Place the photocopies on a cutting mat and carefully cut out the shapes with a craft knife, cutting along the outside edge of each design.

►

Materials and Equipment You Will Need
2.5cm (1in) flat sable paintbrush • Acrylic gesso • Joined and sanded frame • Fine and coarse-grade abrasive paper •
Cork sanding block • Yellow ochre pigment • Photocopied designs • Cutting mat • Craft (utility) knife • No. 2 round sable paintbrush •
Watercolour paints • PVA (white) glue • Spray lacquer • 2.5cm (1in) lacquer paintbrush • Shellac • White spirit (alcohol) •
Wet-and-dry paper • Soft cloths • Metal polish

4 Using the No. 2 round sable paintbrush, carefully paint the photocopies with watercolour paints.

5 Glue the photocopied cut-outs to the frame with PVA glue. Press them down carefully to remove air bubbles.

6 Once the glue is dry, apply a coat of car spray lacquer over the cut-outs. This will prevent the painted photocopies from bleeding into the coloured frame.

7 When the lacquer is dry, use the lacquer brush to apply successive layers of shellac to the frame, allowing each coat to dry before applying the next. When the paper photocopies are buried below the shellac, you have applied enough; usually ten coats will be sufficient.

8 Once the shellac is completely dry, rub the frame down with white spirit. Use wet-and-dry paper and the cork sanding block if the frame is flat, then use a finer wet-and-dry paper. Wipe off excess white spirit with a dry cloth. Apply a small, pea-sized amount of metal polish on to a cloth and polish all around the frame. Buff up the frame with a clean, dry cloth to finish.

LEAD FRAME

This highly unusual frame is very striking and allows you to see all of the framed object, in this case a feather. It is advisable to use this framing method only for small or lightweight objects, as with time the self-adhesive lead tends to move. For a more decorative effect, gild the glass as in the Verre Eglomisé project, distressing the gold (or silver) leaf so that the framed object is visible.

1 You will need two identically sized pieces of glass that have been cut following the method described in Basic Techniques. Clean the glass thoroughly with a cloth dipped in methylated spirits.

2 Measure the wood fillets against the sides of one piece of glass and mark with a pencil where they are to be cut.

3 Once the fillets have been measured and marked, cut along the pencil line with a craft knife on a cutting mat. Alternatively, use a hacksaw with a thin blade.

Materials and Equipment You Will Need
Glass • Cloth • Methylated spirits (methyl alcohol) • 5mm (¼in) thick wood fillets • Pencil • Craft (utility) knife • Hacksaw (optional) • Cutting mat • Thick black felt-tipped pen • Epoxy resin glue • Bradawl or awl • Nylon thread • Feather or other lightweight object • Protective gloves • Scissors (optional) • Self-adhesive lead • Plastic tool • Self-adhesive hangers

4 Colour the fillets all over with a thick black felt-tipped pen and put aside.

5 Using epoxy resin glue, stick the fillets on three sides of one piece of glass, leaving the top section open.

6 Using a bradawl or awl, make a small hole in the remaining fillet and pass a length of nylon thread through it. Secure this with a knot.

7 On the other end of the nylon thread, stick the feather with epoxy resin glue.

8 Place the feather in the frame and stick the top fillet to the glass. Place small drops of epoxy resin glue on to all fillets, then place the second piece of glass on top. Leave to set for 10–15 minutes with a weight on top.

9 Wearing protective gloves and using scissors or a craft knife, cut self-adhesive lead strips to the size of the glass edges, just overlapping the edge.

10 Warm the lead strip in the palm of your hand for a few seconds (which will make the glue on the self-adhesive lead become more tacky). Remove the backing strip, place the lead strip on to the frame edges and apply pressure with a plastic tool. Trim off the excess using a craft knife. Continue all around the frame. Place self-adhesive hangers on to the back of the frame to complete.

OIL-GILDED FRAME

Gilding is a traditional technique that looks magnificent on many wooden surfaces. Patience is required when handling gold leaf for the first time, but the results are definitely worthwhile. In this project, 23¾ carat Italian gold leaf was used on both the frame and the glass, linking the two together very effectively. In spite of the delicacy of the gold leaf, this form of gilding is extremely hardwearing.

1 Paint the frame with several coats of ultramarine gouache paint, allowing each coat to dry completely before adding the next. Draw a design on the frame with a white chinagraph pencil.

3 Place the gold leaf on to the gilder's cushion. Cut it into squares of the appropriate size with a gilder's knife.

5 Carefully place it on the oil-sized design. Leave to dry for 20 minutes more, then gently press the gold leaf down with cotton wool.

2 Using a No. 2 oil paintbrush, apply the oil size to the marked design. Leave the size to dry for 15–20 minutes. It should then be slightly tacky.

4 Brush the gilder's tip on your hand or the side of your face, then pick up the gold leaf with the tip.

6 After 15–20 minutes, gently wipe off the excess gold leaf using a No. 4 round sable paintbrush or a small pad of cotton wool.

Materials and Equipment You Will Need

Paintbrush • Ultramarine gouache paint • Frame • White chinagraph pencil • No. 2 round oil paintbrush • Oil size (30 minutes drying time) • Gold leaf (loose) • Gilder's cushion • Gilder's knife • Gilder's tip • Cotton wool (cotton balls) • No. 4 round sable paintbrush

VERRE EGLOMISÉ MIRROR

Verre eglomisé is glass that has been decorated using gold or silver leaf. The technique is named after an 18th-century art dealer, Jean-Baptiste Glomy, who specialized in gilded glass, but the technique dates back to the Romans.

1 Using the paintbrush and wearing rubber gloves, apply the metal polish to the frame. Dab the sponge over the polish as you work along the frame for a textured finish. Leave for 30 minutes. Apply a second layer of metal polish, again sponging as you work along the frame. Leave overnight to dry thoroughly.

2 Apply a coat of black patina over the frame, wiping it off as you work. The patina will remain in the recessed areas, giving the impression of age.

3 Leave the frame to dry overnight, then polish the entire frame with a burnishing tool for a soft sheen.

4 To make the mirror: clean the glass thoroughly to remove all dirt and grease, using a cloth dipped in methylated spirits.

5 Place half a gelatine capsule in a glass bowl and add a little boiling water. When the capsule has completely dissolved, add 300ml (½ pint/1¼ cups) cold water.

6 Place the glass at an angle of 45 degrees in a tray, so that the solution can run down freely. Cut the gold leaf into small squares. Using a 2.5cm (1in) flat sable paintbrush, apply the solution to the glass, then immediately place the gold leaf on the solution using the gilder's tip.

▶

Materials and Equipment You Will Need

2.5cm (1in) flat oil paintbrush • Rubber gloves • Metal polish • Joined and sanded frame • Sponge • Black patina • Burnishing tool • Glass • Cloths • Methylated spirits (methyl alcohol) • Gelatine capsules • Glass bowl • Deep tray • Gilder's knife • White gold leaf (loose) • Gilder's cushion • Gilder's tip • 2.5cm (1in) flat sable paintbrush • Kettle • Cotton wool (cotton balls) • Pumice powder (0003 grade) • Safety mask • Black lacquer spray

7 Work from the top to the bottom of the glass. Continue until you have gilded all of the glass, then leave to dry. When the gold leaf is shiny, it is dry. If it is matt (flat), it is not yet dry.

8 To seal the leaf, hold the gilded glass about 20–25cm (8–10in) away from the steam from a boiling kettle. Leave to dry once more.

9 Once completely dry, gently brush off any excess gold leaf with a pad of cotton wool.

10 A more distressed, antiqued look is achieved by gently rubbing pumice powder with your fingertips into the white gold leaf. Rub it in using fairly straight strokes.

11 When the desired effect is achieved, brush away the excess pumice powder.

12 Wearing a mask and rubber gloves, spray black lacquer over the ungilded side of the glass. Hold the spray about 20–25cm (8–10in) away for an even coat. Leave to dry.

FRAMING A CANVAS

In this type of frame, the artwork is not placed behind a rebate (rabbet), but instead sits flush with the face of the frame. A gap surrounds the canvas, which gives it depth; the width of the gap depends on personal preference. It is not customary to glaze oil paintings, as they are fairly robust and usually have a protective layer of varnish. Here, the frame is colourwashed to match the colours in the painting.

1 Measure the canvas and add on 5mm (¼in) to the vertical and horizontal measurements. This will give a gap around the canvas when it is eventually inserted into the frame. Measure the depth of the canvas, and choose a moulding that is deep enough to allow the canvas to lie flush with the face of the frame.

2 Mix 2 parts ultramarine gouache paint with 1 part ivory black gouache paint in a glass bowl. Blend together and add 4 parts water. Mix well with a 2.5cm (1in) flat sable paintbrush. This is a very opaque solution. Apply the wash in long, smooth strokes on the face and then the side edges of the frame. Leave to dry for 30 minutes.

3 Turn the frame face down on to a piece of cloth, avoiding damage to the face of the frame. Measure the inside vertical and horizontal edges of the frame. These measurements are for the fillets and the hardboard. Following these measurements, mark and saw the fillets to fit inside the rebate of the frame.

►

Materials and Equipment You Will Need
Tape measure • Canvas • Joined and sanded frame • Ultramarine gouache paint • Ivory black gouache paint • 2.5cm (1in) flat sable paintbrush • Glass bowl • Cloth • Pencil • Wood fillets, 2.5cm (1in) wide, 5mm (¼in) deep • Tenon saw • Hardboard • Black emulsion (latex) paint • PVA (white) glue • Bradawl or awl • 1cm (½in) screws • Screwdriver • Framer's pin gun or panel pins (brads) and tack hammer • Self-adhesive backing tape • Craft (utility) knife

4 Using black emulsion, paint one face and edge of all the fillets and about 5cm (2in) on the edge of the face of the hardboard. Leave to dry. Paint the edge of the canvas.

6 When the fillets are secure, place the hardboard, painted side facing inward, on to the frame and pin into position, using a framer's pin gun, or alternatively use panel pins and a tack hammer.

7 Place the canvas into the front of the frame, lining it up so it is straight. Holding the canvas in position, make a hole in the back of the frame through the hardboard. Insert a screw and screw down with a screwdriver, ensuring that the screw penetrates the wooden batten of the canvas. Repeat in all four corners.

5 Once the fillets have dried, apply PVA glue on to the unpainted side of each one, and place them into the frame.

8 Tape up the back of the frame, covering the pins. Cut mitres in the backing tape, where the tape covers both the moulding and the hardboard.

Lesu redemptor sacculi

O nata lux de lumine

Dignare clemens supplicum

WB

Laudes precesque sumere.

FRAMING A TEXTILE

Whenever you frame a textile, it is advisable to avoid using any form of adhesive, because this will eventually damage the textile irreversibly. The best threads to use are clear nylon thread or, best of all, acid-free conservation cotton thread. The method of decoration used on this frame is a wonderfully simple technique, achieving the look of hand lettering. Any photocopies – from lettering to pictures – may be used.

  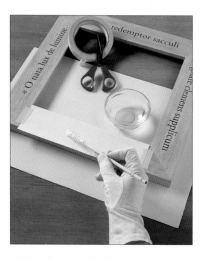

1 Sand the frame first with medium-grade, then with fine-grade abrasive paper. This will produce a smooth finish.

2 Cut the photocopies into strips and place them face down on plain paper, securing with masking tape. Wearing gloves, apply a small amount of silkscreen cleaner on to a piece of cotton wool or a cloth. Gently wipe this on to the reverse of the photocopy. Then, using a dry piece of cotton wool or a soft cloth, wipe over the photocopy again. This will transfer the photocopied text on to the plain paper in reverse.

3 Place the reversed photocopy evenly on to the frame and secure with masking tape. Using a small amount of silkscreen cleaner on a swab, gently apply this on to the photocopy. Then, using dry cotton wool, gently wipe over the photocopy. Remove the applied photocopy and leave the frame to dry for 10 minutes.

▶

Materials and Equipment You Will Need
Frame • Medium- and fine-grade abrasive paper • Photocopies • Scissors • Plain paper • Masking tape • Rubber gloves • Silkscreen cleaner • Cotton wool (cotton balls) or soft cloth • Car spray lacquer • Safety mask • Mounting (mat) board or barrier board • Craft (utility) knife • Cutting mat • Ruler or straight edge • Textile • Pencil • Sewing needle • Eraser • Nylon thread

4 Continue transferring lettering all around the frame in this way, until completed. Wearing a safety mask, apply a coat of car spray lacquer, holding the can about 20–25cm (8–10in) away. This will seal the applied lettering.

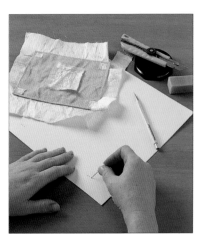

6 Make pinpricks with a needle in the board, then erase the pencil marks.

7 Thread the needle with nylon thread and sew the textile on to the board. Do not sew too tightly, as this may pull and stretch the fabric. A stronger needle may be required when sewing on to mounting board, as it is thicker than barrier board. A leather needle is good for this purpose.

5 Cut out a piece of mounting board or barrier board 2.5cm (1in) larger all round than the textile. Lay the textile on to the board and mark with the pencil where to sew the securing stitches.

8 To finish, pull the nylon thread through to the back of the board and secure in place with masking tape.

BIRCH-FACED PLYWOOD FRAME

Plywood is a construction material consisting of thin sheets of wood glued together. The grains of wood in adjacent sheets are arranged at right angles to each other, which makes plywood exceptionally strong for its light weight. When sanded and rounded off, plywood makes an unusual and pleasing pattern. You can finish this frame with a coat of Danish oil to create a dramatic three-dimensional effect.

1 With a tape measure and pencil, mark the lengths and widths of the plywood and saw the pieces to length. Butt the plywood pieces together to check that they fit well. Cut the back of the frame and set aside. Sand down all the edges.

2 Apply PVA glue to the side edges of the horizontals and strap gaffer tape around the frame, both front and back. Wipe off excess glue with a damp cloth and leave overnight to set.

3 Once the PVA glue has set, remove the tape. Using the cork block and coarse-grade abrasive paper, sand the face and all edges of the frame. This will reveal the dark and light layers of wood within the ply. For a smooth finish, sand again with fine-grade abrasive paper.

▶

Materials and Equipment You Will Need
18mm (³⁄₄in) birch-faced plywood sheet: 2 front verticals, 60 x 6cm (24 x 2¹⁄₂in); 4 front horizontals, 13 x 7cm (5 x 2³⁄₄in); Back, 60 x 25cm (24 x 10in) • Tape measure • Pencil • Tenon saw • PVA (white) glue and brush • Gaffer tape • Scissors • Cloths • Cork sanding block • Coarse- and fine-grade abrasive paper • Danish oil • Rubber gloves • Fabric • Ruler • Craft (utility) knife • Heavy weights or G-clamps • Tack hammer • 2.5cm (1in) large-headed nails • Epoxy resin glue

4 Place some Danish oil in a dish. Wearing rubber gloves, apply the oil over the wood in a circular motion using a soft cloth. Work the oil well into the wood. Buff up with a clean soft cloth.

5 On the back part of the frame that will face the front, apply a line of PVA glue, about 3cm (1¼in) in from the edge. Stick the fabric on to it.

6 Once the glue has set, trim off excess fabric using a ruler and craft knife.

7 Apply PVA glue on to the back of the front section, then place this section on to the fabric-covered section.

8 Place heavy weights or G-clamps on all four corners and the middle section. Wipe away excess glue with a damp cloth and leave to set overnight. Place a cloth below the weights or clamps to prevent damage to the face of the frame.

9 When the glue has set, apply a coat of oil on the side edges of the back section of the frame. Mark out the centre of each window and hammer in a large-headed nail, leaving about 1cm (½in) showing. Mix a small amount of epoxy resin glue and apply this to the nail heads. Place the object on top and leave to set.

RECLAIMED TIMBER FRAME

Reclaimed timber has a natural distressed and heavy appearance, and is one of the easiest frames to construct. Its ample depth allows for plenty of creative three-dimensional effects. This frame requires no finish, relying instead on the natural characteristics of the wood for its rugged appeal. As with any heavy frame, it is advisable to use strap hangers and to hang it directly on to screws placed in the wall.

1 Measure and mark with a pencil the length and width of the verticals and horizontals. Saw with the tenon saw to the correct sizes. Lightly sand the sawn edges.

2 Cut the hardboard to size. On one side apply fabric glue, then stick down a piece of black felt on top. On the other side stick down a piece of decorative paper. Mark out corner holes for the screws, using chalk.

3 Turn the lengths of timber face down and butt them together at the corners. Place the felt-covered hardboard on the back of the timber. Make holes in the hardboard with a bradawl or awl, then screw into the back of the frame, keeping the frame still. The screws will hold the frame together.

4 Turn the frame the right way up, and nail in the corner brackets, using galvanized nails.

5 Cut small fillets to size, coat with PVA glue, then place below the framed object to give a three-dimensional effect.

Materials and Equipment You Will Need

Reclaimed timber: 2 verticals 62 x 10cm (25 x 4in); 2 horizontals, 18 x 10cm (7 x 4in) • Tape measure • Pencil • Tenon saw • Abrasive paper • 54 x 28cm (22 x 11in) hardboard • Fabric glue • Black felt • Decorative paper • Chalk • Bradawl or awl • 14 x 2.5cm (1in) screws • Screwdriver • 4 reclaimed brackets • 8 x galvanized 2.5cm (1in) nails • Hammer • 5mm (¼in) deep wood fillets • PVA (white) glue and brush • Object for framing

PENWORK FRAME

Penwork was one of many artistic amusements popular at the end of the 18th century. Its inspiration comes from India, and it imitates the craft of ivory carving where the design was wiped over with black pigmented wax, which remained in the recesses of the carving while the surface of the ivory remained white. This elegant black-and-white cassetta frame is created by painting the frame solid white, using gesso to cover the bare wood, then transferring a traced design on to it in black ink.

1 Brush acrylic gesso in long strokes along the entire frame, first the face section and then the edge. Allow to dry for about 20 minutes, then repeat. A minimum of four coats of gesso is required. Sand the gesso with medium- then fine-grade abrasive paper to achieve a smooth surface. Apply four layers of white acrylic paint over the frame, allowing each coat to dry for about 5–10 minutes before applying the next.

2 Place tracing paper over your design and trace with a 2B (#2) pencil or use the templates at the back of the book. If necessary, place masking tape on the tracing paper to hold it steady.

3 Place the tracing, pencil-side down, on the frame, and secure with masking tape. Using a 4H (#4) pencil, draw over the design. This will transfer the pencil design on to the frame.

4 Remove the tracing paper and ink over the design with a fine black felt-tipped pen. Paint the rebate (rabbet) with black emulsion or ink it in.

5 When the penwork is completed, wear a safety mask and spray clear lacquer over the frame to seal, holding the can about 20–25cm (8–10in) away. Leave to dry for 5–10 minutes. One coat of lacquer will be sufficient.

6 Using a flat lacquer brush, apply four layers of shellac over the frame, allowing each coat to dry for about 30 minutes before applying the next. This will give an aged ivory appearance.

Materials and Equipment You Will Need

Paintbrush • Acrylic gesso • Joined and sanded frame • Medium- and fine-grade abrasive paper • White acrylic paint • Tracing paper • Design (template) • 2B (#2) pencil • Masking tape • 4H (#4) pencil • Fine black felt-tipped pen • Black emulsion (latex) paint • Safety mask • Clear lacquer spray • 2.5cm (1in) flat lacquer brush • Shellac

TORTOISESHELL FRAME

Tortoiseshell was extremely popular in the 18th century, particularly on hairbrush sets, trinket boxes and small frames. Manufactured plastic tortoiseshell is readily available nowadays, but it tends to look plastic. This method of creating the look of tortoiseshell is fairly realistic, using pigments suspended in shellac. A little time, perseverance and patience are required.

1 Apply yellow ochre oil paint all over the frame, and leave to dry overnight. Apply another coat and allow to dry overnight again.

2 Apply oil size over the face and outer edges of the frame using the flat oil brush. Leave to dry for 15 minutes. When slightly tacky, begin to apply the gold leaf.

3 Place the gold leaf on the gilder's cushion and cut it into appropriate-sized squares or rectangles, using the gilder's knife. Brush the gilder's tip on the side of your face to enable it to pick up the gold leaf. Place the tip gently on the gold leaf and pick it up vertically. Place the gold leaf gently on the oil-sized sections of the frame, without letting the tip touch the frame, then lift the tip up vertically. Repeat all round the frame, until it is completely gilded.

Materials and Equipment You Will Need
Yellow ochre oil paint • 2.5cm (1in) flat oil paintbrush • Joined and sanded frame • Oil size (30 minutes drying time) • Gold leaf • Gilder's cushion • Gilder's knife • Gilder's tip • Cotton wool (cotton balls) • Shellac • 2.5cm (1in) lacquer paintbrush • Pigments: yellow ochre, burnt sienna, Venetian red, burnt umber • No. 2 round sable paintbrush • White spirit (alcohol) • Fine-grade abrasive paper • Cloths • Metal polish

4 Once the frame is gilded all over, let it dry for 20 minutes. Gently tamp down the gold leaf with a pad of cotton wool. Leave overnight.

5 Using the lacquer brush, apply four layers of pure shellac over the frame, allowing each layer to dry for 30 minutes before applying the next.

6 On a small plate mix 30ml (2 tbsp) of shellac with 1.5ml (¼ tsp) of yellow ochre pigment, using a No. 2 round sable paintbrush. Paint this mixture on to the frame diagonally, leaving gaps for the rest of the pigments.

7 Repeat step 5. Then repeat step 6, replacing yellow ochre pigment with burnt sienna.

8 Apply another four layers of shellac, allowing each to dry for 30 minutes before applying the next.

9 Repeat step 6 with Venetian red pigment. Apply four layers of shellac, allowing each coat to dry completely before applying the next.

▶

10 Repeat step 6, using the burnt umber pigment this time.

12 When the shellac is touch dry, dip fine-grade wet-and-dry abrasive paper into a bowl of white spirit and very gently sand all around the frame, ensuring that the abrasive paper is saturated with white spirit. Be careful not to sand through to the pigmented layers.

13 Wipe off excess white spirit with a cloth. Then apply a small amount of metal polish and polish with another cloth. This should produce a smooth and shiny finish.

11 Apply eight layers of shellac, allowing each layer to dry completely before applying the next. Leave overnight.

14 Polish the entire frame with a fresh clean cloth.

EMILY'S FRAME

For this project, a fairly wide-faced and deep moulding is required due to the oblongs and squares that will be chiselled out. The frame is very unusual and has scope for a wide range of creativity. It is decorated with natural objects, including slate pebbles, which are ideal as they are flat. If you require an opaque effect, decorate the glass following the instructions in the Verre Eglomisé Frame project. Because the decoration is so complex, the artwork is the frame itself, so use it to frame either a strong or simple image.

1 Mark out oblongs and squares on the face of the frame with a ruler and a soft pencil. Do not place the shapes too close to the rebate or the outside edge.

2 Score the pencil marks on the frame with a craft knife and a ruler.

3 Chisel out the squares. Remember to chisel fairly deeply, so that the glass will not protrude from the face of the frame.

Materials and Equipment You Will Need

Joined frame • Ruler • Soft pencil • Craft (utility) knife • Chisel • Cork sanding block • Coarse- and fine-grade abrasive paper • 2mm thick glass • Glass cutter • T-square • Soft cloth • Rubber gloves • Olive green oil paint • Etching spray • Masking tape • Protective mask • Black cardboard • Cutting mat • PVA (white) glue and brush • Slate pebbles and other decorative objects • White chinagraph pencil • Epoxy resin glue

4 When all the squares have been chiselled out, sand the entire frame with the cork sanding block and coarse-grade sandpaper, then repeat the sanding with fine-grade sandpaper.

6 Using a soft cloth and wearing rubber gloves, apply the olive green oil paint over the frame, working it well in.

7 Decorate the glass with verre eglomisé for an opaque effect. Spray some of the glass with a little etching spray so that the objects underneath are still visible. To decorate the glass for the slate pebbles, place masking tape in two strips over the glass and spray on the etching spray in a line down the centre, holding it about 20cm (8in) away and wearing a protective mask. When dry, remove the tape.

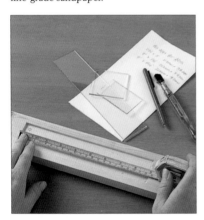

5 Cut all the glass to the sizes required using a glass cutter and a T-square.

8 Cut a piece of black card for the background, apply PVA glue and insert into the chiselled-out space. Mark and cut out card fillets to the appropriate size.

9 Glue the fillets into the chiselled oblong with PVA glue.

11 Glue the glass on to the fillets using epoxy resin glue.

12 Add other decorative elements to the frame as desired. If the objects are flat and small, glue them in the glass with PVA glue, which will dry transparent.

10 Glue the slate pebbles on to the black card background using epoxy resin glue.

TEMPLATES

If the templates need to be enlarged, either use a grid system or a photocopier. For the grid system, trace the template and draw a grid of evenly spaced squares over your tracing. To scale up, draw a large grid on to another piece of paper. Copy the outline on to the second square, taking each square individually and drawing the relevant part of the outline in the larger square. Finally, draw over the lines to make sure they are continuous. Alternatively, two different sizes of graph paper may be used.

RAISED MOTIF FRAME PP54–5
(NOT SCALED)

PENWORK FRAME PP84–5 (NOT SCALED)

SUPPLIERS AND ACKNOWLEDGEMENTS

This list covers a few specialist stores that loaned equipment for photography, and some of the larger online stores.

United Kingdom
Alec Tiranti
27 Warren Street,
London W1T 5NB
Tel: 020 7380 0808
www.tiranti.com

L. Cornelissen & Son Ltd
105 Great Russell Street,
London WC1B 3RY
Tel: 020 7636 1045
www.cornelissen.com

FrameCo – UK
Aylesbury,
Bucks HP20 1BH
United Kingdom
Tel: 020 8144 1658
www.clubframeco.com

Frame Factory
20 Cross Street,
London N1 2BG
Tel: 020 7226 6266
www.framefactorylimited.co.uk

Hobbs & Co.
88 Blackfriars Road,
London SE1 8HA
www.craftsman.me.uk/company-hobbs-co-ltd-in-london-54132

Leonard Villa Framemakers
  and Gilders
316 Caledonian Road,
London N1 1BB
Tel: 020 7700 5010
www.villaframing.co.uk

Metal Paint Ltd
6 Sun Street,
Hitchin SG5 1AE
www.industry.me.uk/
  company-metal-paint-ltd-
  in-hitchin-13679

Robert Randall (Woodcarver)
Unit 1b Hale Wharf,
Ferry Lane,
Tottenham,
London N17 9NF
Tel: 07957 544 491
  and 07932 792 359
www.sandsandrandall.com

Rose and Hollis
G8 Belgravia Works
159–163 Marlborough Road,
London N19 4NS
Tel: 020 7272 5551

United States
Art Materials Service
625 Joyce Kilmer Avenue,
New Brunswick,
NJ 08901
Tel: 888-522-5526
www.artmaterialsservice.com

FrameCo – USA
P.O. Box 929,
Paso Robles,
CA 93446
Tel: 805 624 6687
www.clubframeco.com

framingsupplies.com
1237 Shipp St.,
Hendersonville,
NC 28791
Tel: 800-334-9060
www.framingsupplies.com

Graphik Dimensions Ltd
2103 Brentwood Street,
High Point, NC 27263
Tel: 800-332-8884
www.pictureframes.com

Australia
A1 Framing Supplies
8/104 Newmarket Road,
Windsor, QLD 4030
Tel: 07 3357 3022
www.a1frames.com.au

FrameCo – Australia
20 Trade Place,
Vermont, VIC 3133
Tel: 03 9873 1685
www.clubframeco.com

Marks
Tel: 1300 663 208
www.marksco.com.au/
  framing-equipment

Megawood Larson-Juhl
Central 2B/605 Zillmere Road,
Zillmere, QLD 4034
Tel: 07 3863 8400
www.megawood.com.au

Sydney Art and Framing Supplies
Unit 5/49 Derby Street,
Silverwater, NSW 2128
Tel: 02 9648 1118
www.artandframing.com.au

New Zealand
framingonline.co.nz
14A Shamrock Drive,
Kumeu,
Auckland 0810
Tel: 0800 372 633
www.framingonline.co.nz

Larson Juhl
74–76 Ascot Road,
Airport Oaks 2022,
Auckland
Tel: 09 256 0020
www.larsonjuhl.co.nz

AUTHOR'S ACKNOWLEDGEMENTS
Many thanks go to the following: Andrew Jakeman for his exceptional patience; Paul Jakeman for supplying copious amounts of tea; Robert Randall for just putting up with me; Doreen for her guidance; Nicki for her styling and photography; and Leonard Villa and Jennifer Dinsmore for their valuable knowledge. Special thanks to Ben for many slices of toast and for the use of his computer.

PICTURE CREDITS
The publisher would like to thank the following picture agencies for permission to reproduce their photographs in this book.

Page 8: Jean-Loup Chaumet (top right, bottom left); e. t. archive (bottom right).
Page 9: Bridgeman Art Library (bottom left and top right); e. t. archive (centre).
Page 10: e. t. archive (top); Jean-Loup Chaumet (bottom centre); Bridgeman Art Library (bottom right).
Page 11: Bridgeman Art Library (top); Jean-Loup Chaumet (bottom).

INDEX